Revised and Expanded

poems

Abandoned Breaths

Alfa

Bestselling author of
I Find You in the Darkness

Castle Point Books
New York

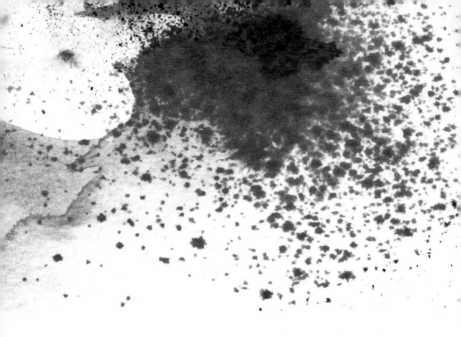

For information, address St. Martin's Press,
175 Fifth Avenue, New York, N.Y. 10010.

www.stmartins.com
www.castlepointbooks.com

The Castle Point Books trademark is owned by Castle Point
Publishing, LLC. Castle Point books are published and
distributed by St. Martin's Press.

Cover design by Katie Jennings Campbell
Interior design by Joanna Williams

ISBN 978-1-250-23357-8 (trade paperback)

Images used under license by Shutterstock.com

Our books may be purchased in bulk for promotional,
educational, or business use. Please contact your local
bookseller or the Macmillan Corporate and Premium Sales
Department at 1-800-221-7945, extension 5442, or by email
at MacmillanSpecialMarkets@macmillan.com.

Originally self-published by AlfaWorldwide.

First Castle Point Books Edition: January 2019

10 9 8 7 6 5 4 3

Contents

Introduction

You are holding *breaths* in your hands.
Can you feel them pulsing?

My intention with this book is to give a
voice to the conversations we've held
prisoner in our hearts for far too long,
the empty rhetoric that plays like
clockwork through our minds, that we
cannot stop analyzing. I've had a
phenomenal response to the book since
first publishing it in May of 2017. Now you
hold the second version, published by
Castle Point Books with the added chapter,
"Vapor." I never imagined that readers
from all over the world would connect so
soulfully with the book's words. What
started out as my sharing *my* abandoned
breaths with the world led to your sharing
yours with me… and I love you all for that.
I hope these words let you know that you
are never alone in matters of heartache
and pain. *You are never alone.*

But, there are words

that need to be said.
They are buried beneath pride and fear.
Rejection has suffocated their
tenacity to bloom.
So, they stay dormant and fester.
Dwelling in the darkest and dusty
corners of a crying soul.
Unseen, yet felt. Not alive, but not dead.

Abandoned Breaths.

Words that need to be said.

Squall

Exhale

When I finally exhaled,
releasing pent-up breaths, the pain and
    resentment tore from my seams like baby
    birds springing from their nests…
and my soul soared.

Losing

I have never been able to understand
how losing someone can make you feel so full
   of longing
that your chest risks exploding with every
   forced breath.
Losing should mean gone
or taken away, empty.
But instead, every pulse in my body
incessantly screams his name. The past
   strangles me at night. It comes blanketed
   in remorse.
Hands of regret crushing my spirit. Waves of
   nostalgia knocking the wind from a chest
   that is much too full
of heirlooms and knick-knacks.
I hold memories of me and you.

Vintage

I believe the pain we experience with endings
    is a tool.
We can use it either to rebuild or to tear
    ourselves apart, piece by piece.
I choose to re-purpose the unhinged parts
    of my soul.
I will let them shine. Rusty and antiqued.
I battled for them. Good versus evil.
    Me against myself.
I may look a little old and worn.
But, my God… run your fingers over my ridges.
Feel my spirit pulse.
You will find character, resilience,
    and fortitude.

I Never Wanted to Change You

I do not want to change you.
Your sadness does not scare me.
If anything, it highlights the fact that you
    are real, and you feel things deep enough,
until they escape your heart and show in
    your eyes,
and I so desperately want you to feel me
that way.

AWOL

He never really had a chance.
I have always viewed relationships through
    rose-colored glasses—the ones my father
    shattered the day he left.
I learned as early as a squalling newborn
    that even the ones who helped
give *life* to your soul…
eventually leave.

Window Shopping

He was a window shopper,
and that is a fine way to spend a relaxing
   Saturday afternoon, but my heart was tired
of being peeked at.
My heart didn't want to be the reason for
   buyer's regret;
it wanted to be *the reason*. All his reasons.

Goodbye Dance

You think the pain goes away?
It does not.
It is always there, lurking.
It is powerful because it has been forged
    by your tears.
It feeds off your memories. It is waiting until
    it sees you dancing in happiness
before it tries to cut in for a waltz.
Do not deny it.
Give it a turn
around your heart's dance floor.
You are stronger now… you can handle
    the beat.
Hold it close. Remember the agony. Kiss it on
    the cheek, and kiss it goodbye.

Memory Bath

There are days
I want to dip my soul
in memories and let it soak.
Then there are other days when I am *praying*
they will all be washed away.

Visceral

He has wanderlust in his veins.
His heart is always seeking, filling up
    on the next adventure. And the most
    painful lesson
I have had to learn
is that you cannot tether yourself to a soul
    that is meant
to fly.

The Artist

He dipped his hands
into my soul, and *finger-painted*
hopes and dreams,
and fears and strengths, into a work of art.
So now it hangs
in a time-suspended display, signed by a
    masterful talent, seeking the right home.

Nocturnal

You have lived in the dark
for so long
that you have forgotten;
a soul needs *light*
in order to grow.

Fairytales

I was spoon-fed fairytales
and rocked on the knees of selfless love
    from birth.
Imagine my surprise when I had to learn the
    hard way that the world won't love you
    like that.
So, you grow up… you face "reality,"
and every beat of your heart asks to go home.

Betrayal

It is in the constant murmur,
the echoes of *never again,*
the hum of betrayal. Vibrations so intense
    their frequency replicates
my heartbeat.
It is in the insistent aching that you feel
    pain
pin-pricking your spine, more so than the air
    filling your lungs.
Betrayal…
is the emptiness you feel when you analyze
    the gaps that your heart stumbles over.
    It pauses—skips a beat,
and with every silent interval, the memories
    flood
and the gaps widen, and betrayal hums.

You Want Him to Miss You...

...to catch a scent on a sun-dappled spring day
  that reminds him of you...
and you want it to cut him in half.
Bring him eye to eye with his weak knees,
with a machete to the heart. You want him
  to ache,
like you have done all winter.
You want him to *endure* what the absence of
  you feels like, and you want it to
last for every minute hereafter because you
  are not someone who is easily gotten over.
And you want him to miss you.

Weightlifter

And my soul spoke to me one day. I heard her
    voice loud and clear, firm, and full of love.

You question your strength…
and I stand by and watch in awe
as you carry that
heavy heart around.

Observation

She wants you to see things
she has never shown you. She hopes you hear
   things she has never said.
She aches for you to spoon her heart outside
   of your bed.

Surreal

My mind is strong.
A steel trap.
I have conditioned myself to let nothing
    escape its confines. I harbor a soul filled
    with eons' worth of strength,
forged and scribed by the Universe. I am a
    celestial wonder,
an endurance hurdler. But when he touches me,
    moves in close...
skimming my world with a gentleness I have
    never encountered before,
I feel a calming need to be still, to quit
    flaying my insecurities
or trying to *prove* my worth.
I want the softness, I need the quiet: I need to
    absorb his essence,
the biting along my armor, and figure out
    how this being has become sustenance to
    my soul.

Emptiness

How do you explain
the absence of a person
to your soul? How do you break the news that
    it may never be whole again?

Invisible

The line between
love and hate is never as faint
as when someone chooses to
leave you.

Recess

And he kept coming back.
Sadly, he was more dependable *when* away,
    and every time she was left to wonder
    for how long.
The signs were always there, mocking her
    heart.
Always knowing the desire would wane after
    he'd had a few bowls of ice cream.
His attention was that of
a boy.
She kept hoping the next time he came back...
he would be
a man.

Brass

Time
has been able to do what I never could
to your memory. It has dulled your shine.

The One

I am not like the women
your mother warned you about.
I am the one she told you to *wait* for.

Time Warp

We hold onto
"I'm sorry"
with thieving hands and sputtering hearts.
Thinking we have the weekends and holidays...
    and tomorrow.
Thinking we have ample time to share the
    words our souls have hidden.

Mask

I am still in love
with the parts
I believed to be true.
All the lies
that began and ended with *I love you.*

Patchwork Quilt

And when I found myself abandoned
with nothing but memories to keep me company,
I wove each one
into intricate patterns and fashioned a cozy
    patchwork quilt
for my soul to curl up with.
Parts of me are threadbare, and the stitches
    are misaligned,
but it is warm.
And more importantly...it is *home*.

Promises

I
will
write
my
feelings
and
let
them
live
the
life
you
promised
us.

Better or Worse

You never know
what you are getting,
until the person who professes to love you
"for better or for worse," reaches into your
    abominable *worse*, and holds your soul until
    it is *better*—
Then,
then, you will know what you have.

Complexities

Tell yourself that I failed you
if that makes the hurt easier to handle,
    because in a way, *I guess I did.*
I failed to understand the complexity
    in loving
someone who would rather walk away than
    stand strong and stay.

Prideful

I have never been jealous
of an emotion before…
but he holds on to his pride with more ferocity
than he ever held on to me.

All of Me

We give so much credit to hearts.
We acknowledge their reckless capacity to love
    with every labored breath,
but I want you to know… my *mind* loved him too.

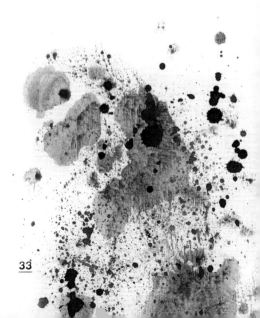

Heroic Love

But if you would have asked me
to take your hand…
I swear, I would have held on
with my superpower.

Monsoon

Journey

To occupy this heart,
you must first pull the weeds that will
    obscure your view.
The walk may be a bit overgrown from neglect.
    At times, you will wonder if you are on a
    foolish pursuit, looking for something that
    does not exist...
but I promise you,
if you make it to the door,
I will answer.

Tangible

How do you look at the minutes
I have given you, and think you know my *years*?
I am overflowing with passion.
I seep memories and slow dance with
    opaque ghosts.
I write things that howl heartache, when my
    soul is merely singing.
I *burn*...but I never catch *fire*.
My touch is substantial, but chances
    are you will
never feel me.

Cleansing

I am learning to embrace my tears.
What I used to look at as a nuisance is now
    a constant reminder
that I *feel...*
and I feel this world and all its vastness,
personally, and painfully.
I am empathetic and caring.
I am absorbing and transparent. I will not
    be ashamed for feeling *until I am full*
    and overflowing.
My tears are necessary. They let me know...
I'm alive.

Battle

The end of us
was like coming home from war.
I know now we were on opposite sides, and
    it was a cause *you* did not believe in
    fighting for.

Deserter

You think you dodged a bullet
by leaving me.
The truth is
you are a deserter… who ran
from the battle of love.

Search and Rescue

It happens.
One day you will meet someone,
and with everything in you,
you will find yourself trying to warn him.
Trying to spare him.
But this one is different.
He does not run.

"I'm deep.
Therefore, you can't wade in the kiddie pool
and expect to find me."

Leaving

You left me
standing there dancing all alone. You walked
    right off the floor... left me twirling,
    gasping for air, lips parted, tongue tied,
refusing to believe you were walking out
    the door
for the last time.
Is this how you dance? Alone?

Season of the Monsoon

It took
time and distance before she was able to
     see herself through calm eyes that were
     no longer clouded
by his darkness.
The wrenching winds
were miles away.
His monsoon would never color her life
     gray again.

Testimony

You think you were born this way...
A pile of rubbish, decaying with every touch.
You have more questions than you have ever
    had answers, and life has not turned out
    how you once imagined it would. You think
    about the past, and it seems you have lost
    more battles than you have won.
But, you were not born with bones of defeat.
You were not singled out in the womb for
    despair. Roll those shoulders back and puff
    out that soul.
You were carefully stitched together with
    breathtaking intention,
With talents and creativity in every
    iridescent thread.
You are a living testimony of resilience...
That you *choose* to rise another day, wearing
    full emotional armor strapped in place *and*
    fight what comes your way, proves that you
    have acquired the strength of a warrior.
    Wear your battle wounds with pride and
    keep on inspiring the world to never
    give up.

I Had a Funeral

I am still in love
with the *possibilities* I had no choice but
to bury.

Tongue Tied

You might
have stayed forever
if I had let my heart speak as freely as my
    spine did.

Heartbreak Hotel

I will always make room
in my heart for you.
You go away—I clean rooms,
in hopes of removing your scent.
Then you come back for an extended stay,
    playing house.
You like the comfortable bed, the soft sheets.
My pliable heart holds your fascination for
    a while.
I am your getaway, your go to.
And as I tell myself *never again,*
I know in my heart,
I will always have an extra bed,
if you need a place to lay your head and be
    loved again.

Afterglow

There we stood,
both trying to put out the fires burning out
    of control in our lives. Somehow, we met
    among the outskirts of the carnage
and found strength in each other...
and we began to slowly sweep the ashes away.

Intuitive

No words were ever said.
It was simply a look. A knowing look that let
    me know
he saw through my facade.
He knew that under *all the toughness*, dwelled
    a woman
who was soft and supple.
A woman he wanted
to touch and never let go.

Mr. Wolf

You think you are so deep and mysterious,
and that you spare me by keeping a distance.
You drop just enough breadcrumbs to keep me
    on your trail,
yet warn me over and over not to get too close
    to the big bad wolf. *I find it really tiring*
    as far as bedtime stories go.
I have been writing your saga for years, and
    besides your verbal account, you possess
    no more demons than anyone else who has
    walked the Earth.
It has been said the loudest and most boastful
    person
in the room is but a fool, while the silent
    person contains wisdom. I know you have
    been to Hell and back, and I could tell you
    what cubicle you rested your head in.
I know your fears as well as you do.
I have been writing your story for years...
    remember?
Just as you tell it. Line after line of drama
    and heartache. But, let me assure you that
    you need not spare me.
While you have always been a star in that deep
    fathomless sky,

I have been the Universe of darkness that
    clutches and holds you in its center. I have
    used your bit of light to help me find my
    way in that massive void.
So, when you worry about subjecting me to your
    darkness, Mr. Wolf,
I worry if I can contain myself from
    swallowing you whole.

Mind, Body, Soul

I feel your pain, and to this day
I have to stop myself from reaching out.
It is second nature to me
to want to comfort your soul.
You want me to put my absence
into terms your heart can understand, but how
    can I do that when my presence never sated
    your hunger?
I wanted you... mind, body, and soul.
Yet, you held back, stubbornly refusing to
    subject me to your Hell. And what you need
    to know
is that Hell was never found
in loving you, but I have lived there since the
    day you pushed me away.

Indelible Ink

Let me try
  to erase
    all the mistakes
      that came before me.

Dieting

And late at night
when you hit me up, telling me you miss me,
   and maybe we should
try again…
I know it is just loneliness and familiarity.
You need instant gratification, and you reach
   for your old
standby.
I am tired of feeding your sweet tooth, and
   then being *expected* to encourage your diet
   the next day.

Intrusion

I hear you knocking,
but I cannot let you in.
The last time almost killed me.
—My Heart

Wondering

I wonder a lot since you've been gone.
I wonder if you are happy;
If you found someone who found the places I
    could not. I wonder if you look at her the
    same way
you looked at me.
I wonder if you are telling her the
    same things
you told me.
But the thing I wonder most of all—
Do you *mean* them this time?

Memories

And if you cut me open,
you will see
that I bleed
memories.

Discovery

My wish is that you will
love him so deeply,
that you will be able to find where he has
    hidden himself. I know I do not have to tell
    you that there is buried treasure there.
But you are about to embark on a search and
    rescue mission, and this discovery could
    set both of your hearts free.

Absent

The irony is,
you are expecting closure from a person
    who would not
even give you his presence.

Worth

I used to be
embarrassed about my broken parts.
Not anymore... even in pieces,
I am worth having.

Patience

She had that look of war-torn terror,
like she had just walked across
an acre of land mines and did not expect
    to live.
She was twitchy when he drew near, and this
    almost broke him.
He wanted to hold her when she got like this,
but he knew if he pushed too hard,
he would most likely send her over the edge.
All he could do
was watch from a distance until she came back
up for air…
and back to him.

Trust Issues

How many people
have to tell you they love
you before you will believe you are
worth loving?

Cold Hard Facts

I simply
revolved around his life, but
he became mine.

Garden of Eden

And all she longed to give away
were the fragrant seedlings that dared
   to grow
in the unkempt garden of her soul.

He Was Magic

He thought he had me fooled
—working me like a tool.
But the reality was I knew
more than I should have, and I turned a blind
    eye, in hopes it would be *me* in the end.

In for the Long Haul

When people would ask her
why she stayed so long,
she usually told them she had stayed until she
    could not take it anymore.
It was simple, and it seemed to satisfy their
    curiosity,
but the real reason she stayed, and kept
    trying, was because she did not want him to
    feel like she had given up on him.
She never wanted to *abandon* him the way she
    had been left
in the past.

No matter if he deserved it...or not.

Puzzle

The thing is,
Love will break you. That is a guarantee.
Yet at the same time, it is the only thing that
can put you back together.

Resignation

Do you see her eyes?
They simmer with the sting of brimstone and
    resignation. She has swallowed heartache,
    and birthed regret.
Yet, her heart still beats among the wreckage.
    She gave all of herself, to the point of
    having nothing left
at the end of it all.

Getting Through

She had no miraculous words
for the souls who thought
she had a magic pathway leading out of
    heartache.
She knew all too well that if you were
    traveling through pain,
you would much rather
quiet the voices
that scream without fail in your head.
She did not tell lost souls they would be okay,
    or that time would heal all wounds.
Instead, she held tight to their hurting
    hearts and outstretched hands,
and tried to help pull them through.

Lyrical Blade

A heart unscathed has never beat to the tune
of a love song.
It is free from the memories that pulse within
the brave and battered souls that have
loved and lost.
As the years go by, memories of lyrics woven
into tendrils of windswept hair will taunt
a heartbroken warrior.
Emotions will surface when recalling
addictive prose once whispered from
misleading lips.
You will be transported with the feeling of
being enveloped within arms
that knew how to hold without withholding and
how it felt to dance while standing still.
The mirage inevitably fades.
The song ends, and with the silence, another
memory surfaces.
The gut-splitting one:
The day he stopped singing your name. And as
the years go by...
You will remember. Over and over. Again.

Stranger

He looks at me as though he has never seen my
  eyes before.
Like he does not remember how they blend in
  with the sky on hot Montana days.
Or the way they tear up when I hear him read a
  bedtime story to a child.
He looks at me, blank face, emotions stripped
  away. A replica of my soul mate.
And I realize a stranger stands before me and
  he is speaking in a language I cannot
  understand.
I can hear my soul ripping in half, and it is
  making his words hard to absorb.
This beautiful man who once told me how many
  freckles I have scattered across skin
that is the softest this side of the
  West Coast…
is looking straight through me.
And even the sound of my heart falling at his
  feet does not startle him
as he tells me he no longer loves me.
And all the while, he is looking at me
as though he has never seen my eyes before.

Warrior

I saw a battleground in his eyes.
The wars he had fought in life held my stare.
He held out his battered hand and cupped
    my face,
and told me he was *utterly lost*.
But I knew that lost was not a place, but was
    a soul
in paralysis, waiting to feel moved, and I
    wanted to help him feel.
And I desperately wanted him to feel me.

More

I am so much more.
More than your shallow heart can hold.
More than your blood that runs cold.
I am more than the
failure you thought I would be.
I am more than the words you spoke to me.
I am more than the reasons you used to flee.
More...
than you will ever let me be.

Obstacles

Be honest with yourself.
You are not afraid to love someone.
You are *afraid*
of not being *loved back*.

Fractured

I often think I am too broken,
not cracked… or chipped, but utterly
     shattered.
Fractured in a way
that cannot be reassembled to the way I
     was before,
but then I look up, and I see the Universe
in all its luminous glow, I know that you can
     still shine brilliantly… even in pieces.

You Are Stardust

Even on the days that you cannot find
one thing about yourself to admire or love,
    I can promise you that you are viewed
    differently by others.
You are unique and effervescent.
You are vintage in a sea of cookie-cutters.
    You are stardust buried beneath self-doubt,
    amazing in ways unequaled,
because your delicate but profound touch in
    this world matters.
No one is you.
You and your heart are leaving lasting
    fingerprints of infinite value… because
    you have perfected the art of loving in
    indelible ink.

You Are Missed

I will always reach for you.
Maybe not with arms, but my mind
grabs hold of you in every memory, and my God,
    its grip is fierce.
You are my motivation
for getting through the day. You have been,
ever since you went away.

Holding On Was Too Easy

I remind myself of my strength often.
At times, I have had to hold on for dear life
    with a coward's grip.
But, if I am honest with myself... the true test
    has always been using my superpower
    to let go.

Zephyr

Story

Learning to navigate a road
you have never traveled
alone
is hard
when you are fleeing the very arms
that pushed you away. I see lost souls
    walking past me.
On the left.
On the right.
All on a mission
to reach happiness. They all have a story.
    They carry it high in their eyes.
Afraid to look at you head on, because
    you might be able to read where their
    hearts have been, and where
they long to go.

Don't Look Back

When I stopped interrogating myself
about what went wrong,
I began attracting everything that was right.

Whispers

I did not look back,
even though the past continued to scream
    my name.
I just ran faster… until all I heard were
    your whispers urging me forward.
    "I don't love you.
It's not you… It is me."

Crawling

I tried to be
what he wanted.
I swear...
I gave it every scream
within my chest. Until one day the cries
   crawled their way out, and led me
out the door.

Buried Alive

I hope you never have to do it.
I hope you never have to bury your soul mate,
knowing they still walk upon this Earth.

Deserving

Any kind of love that is
void of action
is not the kind of love that you deserve.
If you are experiencing the kind of love
that allows them to *willfully* stay away...
    then I beg you, I plead, let it go.
Let them go.
You deserve the kind of love that stays
    by your side,
and does not make you question its existence.

Siren

He ran his hands over my past,
lingering over the dents
and worn edges of my heart.
When I thought he would run away like the
    others had…
He told me I was his siren, and that my heart
    had called to him—
beckoning,
asking him *to bestow*
honor and respect.

Fire

Let's be honest.
We hate our pasts.
Who looks backward and thinks they did
    it right? We made poor choices.
We gave parts of ourselves to people
    who were not
emotionally worthy enough to tie our shoes,
    much less make a relationship a priority.
We allowed them to mistake our kind hearts
    for weak ones. They could not respect us
    because they thought we were drivel,
    pansies, pushovers.
That's what happens when you fall in love.
    Hearts soften a bit.
They tenderize. They rub up against the
    force-fields that have been erected
until they break through—marinated in pain,
    and ready to be thrown into the fire
    of love.

Reflection

You need not worry
if she will make it after you are gone. Her
    track record is testimony to resilience.
What you need to contemplate,
is how her *absence*
will change your life.

Happiness

If there is one thing I know for sure, it is
that the world can be cruel.
It will bare its teeth and you will get your
heart shredded.
Most of the time you will never get the
answers you seek, either.
Prepare yourself... it is going to happen.
To think otherwise is setting yourself up for
a "Why me?" moment.
You cannot *sail* through life.
Yet, whatever you do, do not let it harden you
until your heart is wooden
and splintered beyond repair.
Reinforce self-love because the world will
gleefully snatch it away.
You must know, *deep inside*, that your
existence and contribution matter.
People cannot and will not validate you.
The world will not *celebrate* your uniqueness.
It will not remind you that you are precious
even after toying with you.
So, get used to giving your soul high fives and
long, low whistles.
Happiness *begins* with you.

Twenty-something

I am not twenty-something anymore.
I do not have youth on my side. Wisdom has
    replaced the mistakes, and lessons have
    been disguised as soul fillers.
Perhaps more importantly, the memories have
    been earned; I would not go back and
    change much.
Through heartache, I have unearthed a heart
    that is resilient, and pliant, and deeper
than any five-hundred-page novel I could get
    lost in. My story has been inked with
    mystery, intrigue, deceit, crime, true
    romance…
and too many toxic turns.
All of this has helped create a desire to live
    a life with a passion
that is no longer on hold.

Love Yourself

If I had never visited the darkness,
I would have never found my light.
Learning to *love myself*
was a foreign emotion.
I had to learn to *like myself* first, and it took
    some time to convince my heart,
that I was worth a
second look.

Quiet

Never make the mistake
of thinking a quiet soul is an empty one.

Risen

I hurt in places
you brought back from the dead.
Now I have to lay them to rest again.

Calendars

I know all about scars.
My smile is the mask I wear
365
days
a year.

Human Heart

I will never understand
the vastness of the human heart's landscape.
   How it can hold *centuries* worth of love
within its walls,
yet harbor *lifetimes* of hate in every nook and
   cranny.

Vacant

I kept the door wide open—
not halfway, not a narrow crack, but torn free
    from its hinges.
I kept it open
in case you walked through. Now it is time.
I am locking the door
I have stood and prayed from. I am bolting it
    from the inside.
I can no longer give you permission to visit,
    or to knock on it.

Masquerade Ball

The world is full
of precious souls
wearing masks
to hide the pain.

Illumination

Storms don't scare me,
especially in the middle of the night.
The lightning makes it easier to see
    the ghosts
in the corners of my heart.

Gardener of Heartache

I will always wonder
if I pruned your garden
too closely...
and if that is why you had to leave in order
    to grow.
How barren
would my mind be, if I let you go?

Metamorphosis

What I view as catastrophic,
is in fact a metamorphosis.
I am becoming the *best version* of myself.
Pain has carved the
eighth wonder of the world.
A *Survivor*.

Shaking

My spirit encounters earthquakes,
and nothing soothes its tremors more than
    absolute *quiet*.
Stillness is the comfort I seek
as the Universe rips me wide open in
    quivering despair.
I have come to accept that my soul is shifting.
It is changing and purging… making room
    for growth
and for more love.

Ache

I would rather ache
than feel nothing at all.
To know that I respond
to another heart with such craving
   reminds me that
I am *alive*.

Time Changes Things

I believe in change because
I have watched it manifest within
   my own heart.
It is a process, not an overnighter.
The tough part is enduring the *ripping*
   and the mending.
You cannot go through pain
and not be changed *in some way.*
The skeletons come out of the closet,
   and dance
with your hopes and dreams, and the
   best version of yourself is the
   last man standing.

Queen of the Jungle

There are those who mistake
her sorrowful eyes for weakness. What they do
   not understand is that supernatural
   strength grows from pain,
and that this soft and delicate creature
who purrs like a kitten is really a woman
with superpowers who roars with the ferocity
   of a lioness.

Missing

For so long,
I believed in darkness, and darkness alone.
The black void that I had sentenced my heart
    to live in had become my home.
My refuge. It was safer that way, because when
    I allowed myself to *feel*,
I did not have to open my eyes while
    swallowing darkness,
—and I did not want to see what I was missing.

Fracture

My heart hurts for those
who have been broken so badly, and are so
    irreparably fractured, that they do not
    believe *magic* exists.
How I wish they could feel my earth shift when
    he looks at me. Then they might…
They might believe, *again*.

Letting Go

Why do we hang on to the broken ones?
The broken words—the ones never released.
They are the ones you remember with
    absolute clarity.
You can't remember what you had for breakfast,
    but you will remember conversations and
    the cutting retort you never released.
Those carefully rehearsed sentences take on a
    life of their own,
cutting off your blood supply and throbbing
    with arousal.
They become bigger than life inside you and
    grow more resentful with age.
Until one day... one day you find a way to let
    them live *outside* of you.

Screaming

The past visits at night,
cloaked in alluring familiarity. It wraps
    its seductive hands disguised as
    diamonds around
my throat.
The pain always comes draped in sighs dressed
    as memories—rousing my spirit. Waves of
    nostalgia knock the wind from a heart
    on lockdown.
It is always at night, when my bedroom is the
    color of my inkwell, that I
talk to the shadows waiting in the room.
    The walls creak and moan,
laboring and gasping for breath… all the
    while absorbing my agony, storing it for
    another day.
My ghosts feel more at home every day.

Lights Out

Every night is the same.
I swathe myself in inky blackness, thinking
    it will distinguish
the light burning in my soul.
That
is when
the memories of you
continue to illuminate your absence.

Raw

I'm saddened
because I wanted him to see the scrubbed face.
The same one that has too much sun.
I wanted him to see the woman behind the mask
    I wore for society to accept me.
I wanted him to see beneath.
So, when he called me beautiful, having known
    me for minutes,
I knew he had no interest in my years.
His hunger was superficial,
and this soul needed
deep appreciation.

Lost and Found

I found myself
by looking in the mirror, and meeting
a stolen soul, eye to eye.

Roped

Sometimes
it is the ones who love you with intentional
    presence who *win* your heart
in the end.
They are not driftwood, but the docks
To which you affix your soul.

Roots

I needed a man
with tree-trunk feet.
Shallow roots would never do.

Standing Still

I do not have the energy,
nor the will,
to fight with you, or against you, anymore.
I am going to stand still, and let the
    war cries
fly right past me.
The battle may be far from over, but
    in my mind,
I have already won this war.
I will still be standing right here,
    safe and sound,
when your heart gets tired of fighting
    and seeks its way home.

Inner Care

Imagine how lovely
humanity would be
if we focused on making our souls beautiful,
rather than our faces.

Memories Hold You Close

We made it work for a little while.
I take comfort in the fact that for a moment
    in time I had your attention, and the magic
    that held us entranced made us dance amid
    fiery coals.
Whatever the outcome, I will never regret
    taking your hand.
The embers reflected in your eyes
were worth it. The memories, worth it. The
    blisters on the soles of my feet, worth it.
Our breaths dancing close, were worth it all.

Beats of Remorse

And every time you feel your heart
straining
to beat to a rhythm that no longer exists,
I hope it serves as a *constant* reminder of how
    it feels to lose something
that was so precious and taken for granted.

Actions

Emotions are pure
when a person has *everything* to lose.
Watch closely,
and see what they are willing to fight for.
You will know then
what they are passionate about.

Salty Winds

Your words flow like salty winds,
caressing my sweltering heart.
What incantation
have you bound me with as I try to stand,
unable to move these sea legs at your
    approach?
Surely you are half magician,
half siren, as I watch you dance across the
    sands of time,
and into my heart.

Nine Seconds of Heaven

I never knew
what magic felt like
until you cupped my face in your hands
for a full nine seconds before you kissed me.
I felt butterflies
ruffle the edges of my heart.

Collision with No Insurance

I sit back
and I appraise the wreckage. It's like that,
after a storm blows through. You weigh what is
    salvageable against what is lost.
And you hope you find
your heart somewhere within the disarray...
because it's hard to rebuild when
    the foundation
has been ripped away.

Abandoned

He calls it changing your mind.
I call it an intentional lie. He says
    priorities change.
I say people get bored and move on. He says
    it is him,
not me.
I say people will justify their own wants…
so they don't have to stay.

Always Right There

He did not seem to grasp
that if he had stopped running, and looked
    around, I was right there.

Conquest

All he did was breathe life into my soul.
    I was a conquest. An easy one,
    and you don't know how badly it hurts
        to know
        that I was *used*
        and *tried*
        for a time.
        Then thrown back.

Exhalation

Do Over

It is hard to read.
I find myself refraining from trying to reach
    out, direct, or shake them silly.
I've done it. I've done it all already.
Everything I read, I have done. I have lived it.
I realize you are lost
in the same Universe I have traveled through.
You will keep searching the void inside your
    chest until, amazingly, you find the salve
    in the same place you were lost.
The only thing you find on those journeys,
    those nomadic quests you take to try
    to understand
your purpose—and all of humanity and its
    breath you ache to feel—
the only thing you discover about yourself out
    there is *what really matters*.

Love More

The only thing that will be permanently
    etched after a
lifetime of soul chasing will be
whom you let come and go from your life.
When you are close to death and holding
    hands with darkness, trying to make
    sense of it all
for the last time, it is not another drink
you will crave or another city you will long to
    explore. You will wish you had loved more.
Held more. Told more… LOVED more.
That is the regret that will gnaw. You will
    analyze the contents of your underused
    heart,
and you will see it contains oceans of love
    that were never given away.

Hungry

I have always been hungry
for something to fill me, to fill the void deep
    within my chest.
I walk around with this incredible ache.
It's gnawing, growling,
demanding that I give in and feed the craving
    that is never sated. The problem is,
the only thing
that looks appetizing...
is him.

Yearning

I turned to walk away,
and I heard you say my name,
but I did not stop.
I took another step away, and you said
    it again.
This time with such affliction, my heart
    cracked just a bit.
Then you reached for me, and I felt such
    yearning in your hands,
that it was the last straw.
I turned around and held your gaze—
    I was a goner.

Life Force

The air would bend
when he left
the room.

Eyes

One day he told me
I had vibrant eyes,
and it had been so long since I had taken the
    time to look at them, that I
ran to the mirror.
I stood there, mesmerized by a creature I had
    forgotten existed.
I had *lovely* eyes.

Connection

I know you miss me
because that connection we had is still there.
I am choking on the cord. We are still
    attached,
and, *it hurts...*

Submerged

I know you are feeling like
you cannot possibly let it out.
You do not want anyone to think you are crazy,
    so you bottle it up. You think, surely no one
    else could think the thoughts that swim
    through your mind.
I have been swimming in the deep end
for a very long time.
My limbs ache from treading a lifetime of
    waves, and at times I am grow numb.
But I have learned to let it out, even if I come
    up coughing water. I let it out because
    drowning would be far too easy.

Touch

If you can find a way
to make me feel
your love tonight,
then I will promise you
tomorrow.

Latching On

This thing between us,
this intense conversion of souls transforming
    into a single unit,
is quite daunting
if you focus on the power involved.
To witness two singular vessels meld is
    a miracle
in itself, but to feel the tremble as they
    converge and latch on, is a euphoria
    unsurpassed.
Nothing is Love's equal. Nothing.

Runner

Her feet would always start slow,
but gained momentum
as her heart coaxed it along.
The faster she ran,
the more the wind would whip
and fuel her inner reserve.
She was not the kind
of woman to stick around and wait for love to
    break her.
She left while the memories were still
    something she wouldn't mind sleeping with.
She had learned the hard way that pain wasn't
    good snuggle material.
She liked her memories vibrant and full of
    life, like the soul
she had painstakingly restored. No man would
    ever catch her. She ran fast.

I Matter

You think all I live for is the bedtime
romance, and to be swept off my feet. The
    reality is that I only want to know that I
    matter—beyond any shadow of a doubt. That
    is freeing in a way that is indescribable.
    It enables a person to give every last bit
    of the love that is
aching to be set free.

Maintenance

She had a faraway look
in her eyes that begged for closer inspection.
She could take you to faraway kingdoms with
    her well-traveled stare.
If you took the scenic route, you would find
    fragrant fields fraught with
heartache and *what could have been*.
If you delved deeper, past the *pain-filled
    irises*,
you would see a weary traveler, trying
    to navigate
her way back home.
She had perfected the art of looking
    maintained on the outside,
but inside she had really let herself go.

Speed of Light

And the truth is,
you run through my veins
faster than any shooting star.

Afraid

I am not afraid of you.
You do not scare me. What does frighten me
    is the thought of you
bailing out on our one chance at making
    this work.
You are right—
you are so broken,
but, my God,
you are so beautiful.

Waiting

I love you.
Even when you go away, and I hold my breath
until you return.

Moonbeams

When I asked you
to tell me
about the Universe, you replied:
"I taste stars in your mouth. I see galaxies
    in your eyes.
I smell moonbeams in your hair.
I feel space…
without your touch."

Blessed

I saw you looking at me
when you did not think I knew, I saw.
I must be honest, it scared me.
You scared me.
I was not prepared for the softness I saw
   in your eyes.
If I thought them beautiful before,
they are hypnotic now. How did I get so lucky
   as to have your eyes
land on mine
and not look away?

Anchored to You

You need not worry.
My heart will never wander. It is tethered
    and tied, wound tight.
It is anchored at the cove where shelter
    was offered.

Warrior

He has one thing
on his mind,
and that is to carry her
as far as she will let him.

Treasure Trove

She tried to explain the
contents of her heart to him.
Her heart spoke up midway through,
and told her it should not have to be
    explained
to the person
who should *treasure* it.

Dreamer

She was a dreamer with a penchant
for transcendental thinking.
A woman who believed in the same magical love
    that romance novels try in vain to capture
    and portray in all its lustful allure.
She scoffed openly at the naysayers, the
    stone-faced hardened souls who told her
    fairytales do not exist.
Her heart was not a prison, surrounded by
    barbed wire, nor was it a desolate, barren
    place.
It was an open field she visited daily;
running free among furry dandelions.
And there
she wished her dreams into reality.

Thank You

As much as I hate giving him
any more of me,
 I must thank him for the trials.
Without them, I would not have acquired my
    survival skills.
I would never have been able to climb out
    of the valley.
The view up here is so much more serene.

Marrow

You have far too much love
stored in your bones to use it on past loves.
Save some for your future.

Emerald Cut

She's been through more hell
than you'll ever know.
But that is what gives her beauty an edge.
You cannot touch a woman who can wear pain
like the grandest of diamonds around
     her neck.

Closed Door

I am not one of those girls
who needed him to say
"It is over" and then explain to me why
   he reached
that decision.
I get my closure by listening to all the things
he did not say while he was walking away.
I could not have handled hearing it twice.

Kingdom

I needed you to see past the
illusion I had tried so hard to create.
Magic is always hidden.
I wanted you to delve deep, to find the stars
    I had named after every dream
I had ever had of you. The skies in my soul are
    vast and the hills hide fairytales.
I wanted you to explore
the kingdom I kept locked away. It is not
    for everyone.
Only those who dare to believe will ever
    find it.

Grind

My soul has teeth,
and there are maddening nights,
like tonight,
when the sound of
its grinding—trying to obliterate the taste
of you, and of what remains—
is really
just too much.

It Was a Gift

Do not mistake
the absence of closure
for a lifetime connection.

Empty Handed

Today is the day.
It hit me.
The buildup of emotions
that we all carry around
exploded.
Tears ran down my cheeks,
and did not stop until my shoulders were
    puddling in remorse.
And you would think that,
after weeping enough liquid
to bathe triplets, I would feel better,
    or relieved.
But the only thing I feel is emptiness of the
    tears I held inside.
I am upset because I could not
hold on to them either.

Not All Endings are Bad

If you look out your window tonight
and see the clouds roll back
to showcase the moon in all its brilliance, you
    will understand why I had to walk away—
so you can shine today.

Favorite Book

You are the story
I chose to write, the pages I've lovingly
    breathed life into,
with punctuation that highlights your moans
    and sighs. Flirtation along the carefully
    crafted paragraphs…
climaxes amid every chapter.

Projection

Like yourself, just as you are.
Accept yourself in your entirety. Let the
    scars heal,
and do not pick at them.
Don't look at people and measure your self-
    love by what they project to make
    themselves happy.
Take a long look.
You don't want their lives anyway. You do not
    like anything they do, say, or portray.
Why, then, have you been so hard on your soul?
Can't you see that you don't deserve
to be treated that way?

New Beginning

You think it is time
for a new beginning.
You long to start from scratch, so you seek
    new interests, experiment with taking
    risks, trying to reinvent yourself.
Out with the old and in with the world's new,
but you will never create a version of
    yourself
that is as magical
and unique as the original.
Never lose yourself...
in an attempt at finding yourself.

Second Round

You are afraid to sever the ties
because you think the same love won't happen
    twice in your lifetime.
And, you are right.
It will not.
No relationship is the same.
You gather bits and pieces
from each one, until the puzzle is complete.
Then you are ready for the real thing.
Never lose hope.
That bad track record made you strong.
    You know what you *do not* want now.
The past was basic training for the real
    thing. Take your stance, and ready
    your heart.
You've got this.

Reckoning

I saw our ending in
a spectacular display
of illumination.
The closure I sought fully delivered
as I stood barefoot, and bereft of emotion
in the headlights of your dismissal.
But I'm not the girl you walked away from.
I am not the heart you threw away.
I am the soul who absorbed the Universe...
    and finally found her way.

Brilliance

I made myself look back,
to relive those years of roaming in
    the darkness.
He had crushed my heart with a heavy hand,
and an even weightier ego.
I reminisced. I dug.
I hacked away through the mines I once felt
    lost in.
I unearthed diamonds in those caverns of my
    soul where there was once only blackness.
I discovered that my past was necessary, in
    order to create the rarity and the clarity
of my self-worth.

Goodbye Blue Bird

I held tight to words
when I should have let them go.
I was handcuffed to *should have* and *what if*
    with taut heartstrings and a strength
    to be envied.
When I finally inhaled the air of poetic
    release,
I absorbed the Universe, and my blue bird
    was gone.

Fragrance of Survival

Take a long whiff of that burning bridge
you dared to ignite with strikes of finality.
That is the scent of survival you smell.
　　Inhale till you are full.
The aroma
is breathtaking, isn't it?

Memorize

He was a novel.
Reading him would never be enough
    for my soul.
So I decided to memorize him.

Seams

I never knew
how deeply
you were
embedded
into my
seams
until I
tried to
split them.

Inked

Our love is immortal.
We have become a love story. I siphoned the
    moments from my heart and soul, and I have
    inked them
into beautifully bound pages.
We live on for another generation to try to
    understand
how the beauty of love
can turn into ugly reality.

Words Heal

And on good days, when the self-love
    is flowing,
and I view myself as *worthy* and
    unforgettable,
I speak to my soul in words meant to soothe
    the ache.
I am loving—because my soul is in dire need,
    yet I am forceful,
because I know it is required.
And when his memory chants its sorrowful
    wail,
I counter with words that are strong, resolute,
    and effective.
"It is my intention to make my leaving an
    event you will never recover from."

Rarity

You think he is the reason for your happiness,
and that your life revolves around him. My
 beautiful star, you are so much more than
 that. You are not a piece of matter floating
 around under his domineering control.
You are a beautiful, charismatic moonbeam in
 a world of dead space.
He's tried in vain to empty you of your wonder.
He's still doing it.
This relationship, this cosmic hell hole
 that you've been thrust into, does not
 own your soul.
It is the cause of your pain—*he* is the cause
 of your pain. So, let him go, and release
 yourself from the binds that hold you
 stagnant in your sorrow.
He wanted you because you were rare in his
 world. And you still are.
Don't you ever forget that.

Legacy

I will never stop writing
my story in ink.
I need to leave my children proof that pain
can be transformed into beauty.

Vapor

Before and After

I'm two different women.
Before him
and
after him.
And they do not
like each other...
at all.

Listening

Ah, but *listening* is so underrated.
Having a man
lock eyes with you
as you're talking.
His inquisitive eyes are immersed
as they watch your mouth share parts of you.
His ears perking and on their mark.
His chest rises and falls, full of *you*.
Listening is one of the most desirable
skills a man can possess.

Collectible

You toy with me.
You wind me up
and set me down
once a week.
You like to see me perform.
I'm a collectible—
something acquired,
but with a value that stops
at your stare, and lies
forgotten until you want
to express ownership.
You want me *in* your life
but *not as a part* of your life.
I am a possession
who is only handled
when I am establishing worth.

Persuasion

Quit trying to convince
your heart,
your mind,
your soul,
and your world,
that you love me.
You should not
have to convince
yourself
to love me.
I am not something
to talk yourself into.

Unscripted

The perfection is found
in the disarray.
In the moments untouched,
unscripted,
unmanufactured.
When you're standing
in the middle
of her chaos…
and you realize
you would not
change
a thing.

Confidence

You watch her walk in
with carefree confidence,
and you wonder how it must feel
to wear *grace* so easily.
But you have no idea
how long she saved
before she could afford
to wear the priceless *peace*
that she had prayed so long for.
You see, nothing comes easy.
Not love.
Not the right man.
Not strength.
And certainly not self-love.

Flicker

The smoke rolls off her shoulders.
Years of carrying
more than her share
have *at last* become too much.
So with matches from the pockets
of his discarded jeans,
she lights his last connection
to her...
in flames.

Grounded

I have never been one to take things lightly.
I love with a
heavy,
heavy,
unmovable
hand.
I love with a locked heart
that is grounded
by the
weight
of time.

Private Lives

My grandma used to tell me to watch how a man
   treats his mother, his sister, and the other
   women in his life.
She said it was a **99%** indication of how he
   would treat you.
But I found out the hard way that a person's
   public demeanor is not always an accurate
   display of the secrets they store in their
   private lives.

He Would Answer

When he doesn't answer, I like to imagine that
    I've taken his breath away. Perhaps he is so
    overwhelmed by the sheer emotion of my
    words that he is rendered speechless.
    A mind can conjure any excuse it sees fit.
But the truth is, if I mattered...
He would answer his primal response to
    something that gives his life sustenance.

Endless

I think of love as a river that flows through
  canals carved in our hearts. It explains
  the endless amount of tears one cries
  when the channels are damned.
I named my river after you. *Endless.*

Again

They will push you out the door
and tell you to *start living again,*
and you have not even begun
to dust the ashes off your shoes
from your last walk
through Hell.

Replacing

Why are we molded into
believing that *replacing* someone
is the only way to get
over them?

Nibble

Don't be like me.
Don't crave the ones who only give you
    a nibble
and always leave you hungry.

Elixir

Tell me why we hold on to people,
places,
and things
that we know are the toxic elixir
to the intentions
of our hearts.
Tell me, and if by some stroke of magic
you make sense,
maybe you can save me.

Acknowledgments

To **Kevin, my children, and my mom,** who have had to endure my quirks and my hermit status—*thank you* for loving me and for learning to love a *writer.* I love you all.

To **Jesus Christ.** You are the reason in *every* season of my life. Thank you for taking me on the pathway that has led me *to today.*

To all my **Readers** on Facebook, Instagram, Tumblr, Twitter, and Pinterest: *Thank you. This is for you.*

About the Poet

Alfa would paint the world in hues of turquoise if she could. Unapologetic about her realistic take on heartache, she writes to let her readers know they are not alone in their pain. Her four children and three granddaughters, the stars of her life, were the catalysts that pushed her to force her words and her smile on the world after a lifetime of depression and anxiety. She wanted to leave something behind for them, a legacy, proof of existence, and proof that pain can be transformed into beautiful inspiration. Alfa lives in Louisville, Kentucky. You can find her on Instagram @alfa.poet